W9-BAG-569

9/30/19 Childs World

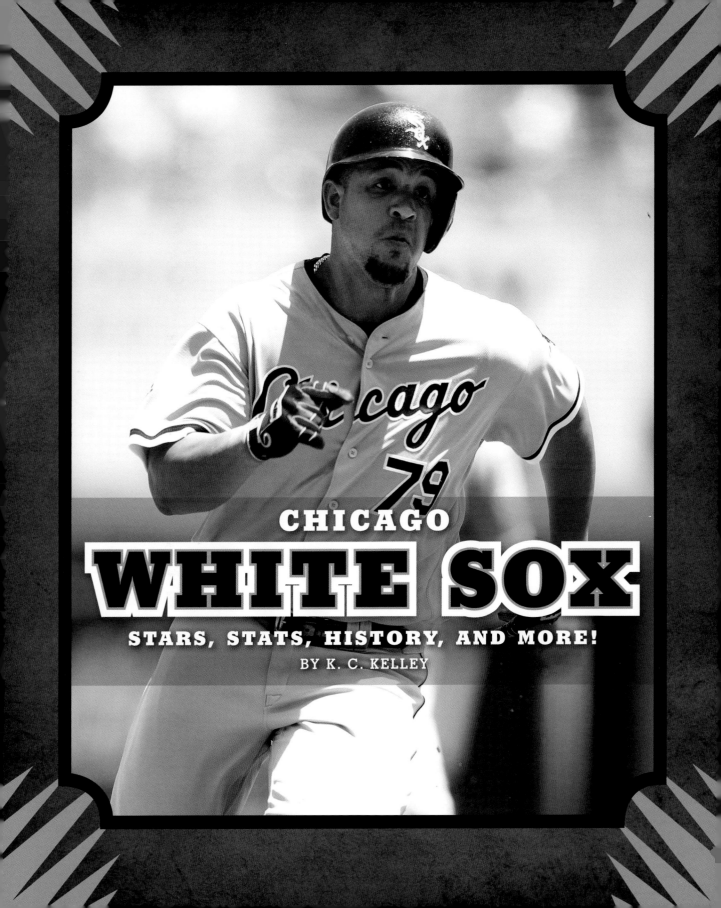

CHICAGO
WHITE SOX
STARS, STATS, HISTORY, AND MORE!

BY K. C. KELLEY

Published by The Child's World®
1980 Lookout Drive • Mankato, MN 56003-1705
800-599-READ • www.childsworld.com

ISBN 9781503828193
LCCN 2018944832

Printed in the United States of America
PAO2392

Photo Credits:
Cover: Joe Robbins (2).
Interior: AP Images/Icon SW 19; Ken Lund/Flickr 13;
Library of Congress 9; Newscom: Nuccio Dinuzzo/KRT
17; Daniel Bartel/Icon SW 20; Keith Gillett/Icon SW 27;
Robin Alam/Icon SMI 29; Joe Robbins 5, 6, 10, 14, 23, 24.

About the Author

K.C. Kelley is a huge sports
fan who has written more
than 100 books for kids. His
favorite sport is baseball.
He has also written about
football, basketball, soccer,
and even auto racing! He lives
in Santa Barbara, California.

On the Cover

Main photo: Slugger Jose Abreu
Inset: Hall of Famer Frank Thomas

CONTENTS

GO, WHITE SOX!

The Chicago White Sox share a city with the Chicago Cubs. White Sox fans cheer in the southern part of the city. Cubs fans are in the north. The two teams are in different leagues. They are still **rivals** for fan attention. White Sox fans have plenty to be happy about, including a World Series win in 2005! Let's meet the Chicago White Sox!

Tim Anderson is one of the exciting young players ➤
who have White Sox fans ready to win!

WHO ARE THE WHITE SOX?

The White Sox play in the American League (AL). That group is part of Major League Baseball (MLB). MLB also includes the National League (NL). There are 30 teams in MLB. The winner of the AL plays the winner of the NL in the **World Series**. The White Sox were baseball's champs in 2005. Their fans are hoping for another title soon!

 Yoan Moncada makes a play for the White Sox on the infield.

WHERE THEY CAME FROM

The White Sox started in 1901. They were one of the original teams in the AL. They are one of only two AL teams to have kept the same name. The other is the Detroit Tigers. The White Sox won the World Series in 1906 and 1917. In 1919, they lost to the Cincinnati Reds. Later, MLB found that some White Sox players had lost that series on purpose! Those players were **banned** from baseball. The team didn't reach the World Series again until 1959!

Shoeless Joe Jackson was a great player who got ➤ caught up in the 1919 cheating scandal.

WHO THEY PLAY

The White Sox play in the AL Central Division. The other teams in the AL Central are the Cleveland Indians, the Detroit Tigers, the Kansas City Royals, and the Minnesota Twins. The White Sox play more games against their division rivals than against other teams. In all, Chicago plays 162 games each season. The team plays 81 games at home and 81 on the road. From 1969 to 1993, the White Sox were in the AL West Division.

◄ *Matt Davidson is one of Chicago's top young hitters.*

WHERE THEY PLAY

In 1991, the White Sox moved into a brand-new ballpark. It was called New Comiskey Field. Charles Comiskey was one of the team's first owners. The stadium replaced "Old" Comiskey Park. The team had played there since 1910. At New Comiskey, when the White Sox hit a homer, the scoreboard sets off fireworks! In 2016, a company paid to name the ballpark **Guaranteed** Rate Field.

The wheels on the scoreboard spin and fireworks ➤
explode when Chicago hits a homer.

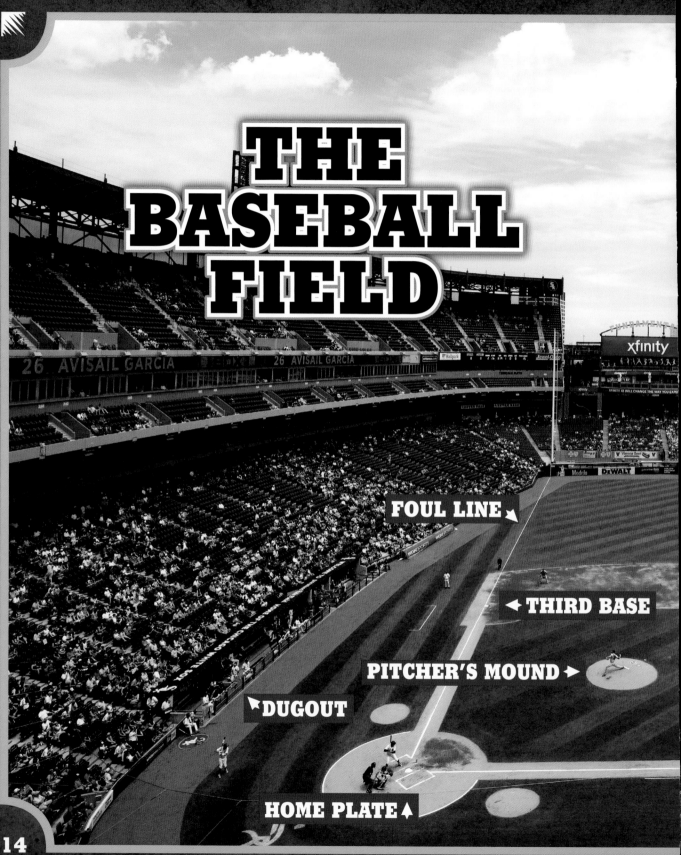

THE BASEBALL FIELD

FOUL LINE ◀

◀ THIRD BASE

PITCHER'S MOUND ▶

▶ DUGOUT

HOME PLATE ▲

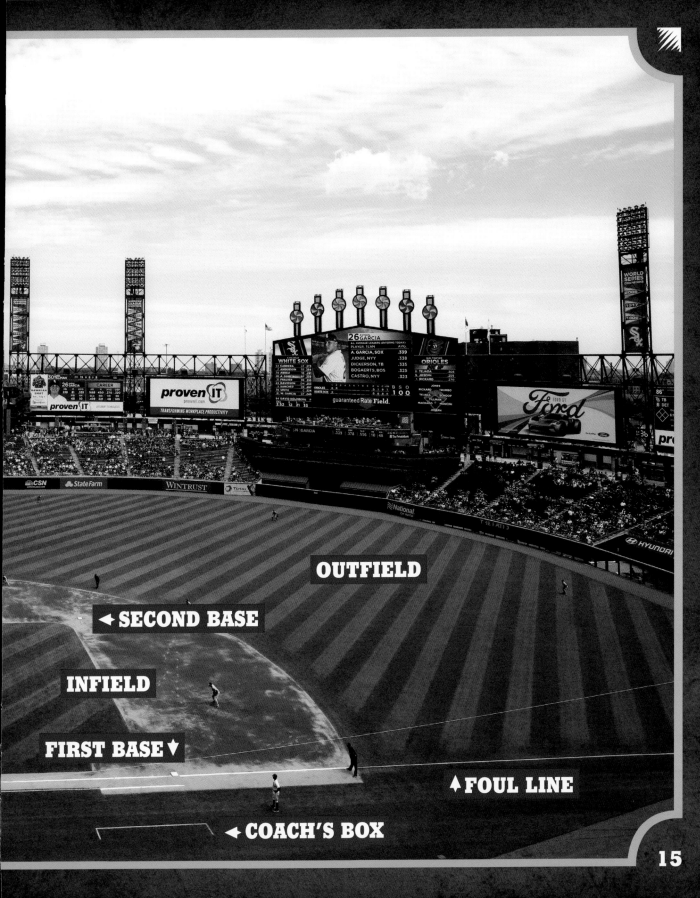

OUTFIELD

◄ SECOND BASE

INFIELD

FIRST BASE ▼

▲ FOUL LINE

◄ COACH'S BOX

BIG DAYS

The White Sox have had a lot of great days in their long history. Here are a few of them.

1906—The White Sox won their first World Series. **Hall of Fame** pitcher Ed Walsh won two games for Chicago.

2005—The White Sox beat the Houston Astros to win the World Series. It was Chicago's first title since 1917!

2012—Philip Humber pitched a **perfect game** against the Seattle Mariners. It was one of only 16 wins in his career.

Time to celebrate! The White Sox jump for joy ➤
after winning the 2005 World Series.

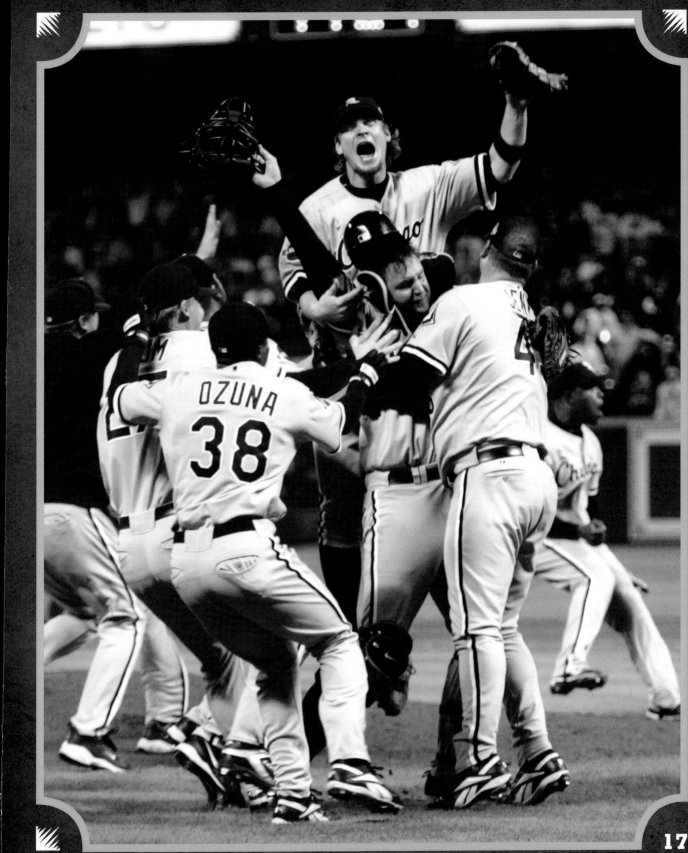

TOUGH DAYS

Like every team, the White Sox have had some not-so-great days, too. Here are a few their fans might not want to recall.

1970—Chicago has had a lot of losing seasons. The worst came in this year. The White Sox lost a team-record 106 games.

1976—The White Sox made their players wear short pants. Most fans and players hated them! The idea only lasted for three games.

2018—The White Sox won only 9 of their first 36 games. It was the team's worst-ever start to a season!

Chicago's owners made the players wear short pants in ➤
1976. This did not go over well with fans or players!

MEET THE FANS!

White Sox fans are called "Southsiders." The White Sox ballpark is on the South Side of Chicago! The fans stay loyal to their team through thick and thin. They love their ballpark's exploding scoreboard. A **mascot** named Southpaw helps fans cheer for the "Chisox" (CHY-sahx).

◄ *Southpaw is another name for a left-handed pitcher. And the White Sox play on the city's South Side!*

HEROES THEN

d Walsh pitched for the White Sox from 1904 to 1916. He once won 40 games in a season! Shoeless Joe Jackson was one of the best hitters of all time. Sadly, some people think he took part in cheating during the 1919 World Series. Second baseman Eddie Collins was a Hall of Famer. He helped Chicago win the 1917 Series. Speedy Luis Aparicio was one of the first superstars from Venezuela. First baseman Frank Thomas won two MVP awards with the White Sox in the 1990s.

Frank Thomas was nicknamed ➤
"The Big Hurt" for what he did to baseballs.

HEROES NOW

José Abreu is following in Frank Thomas's footsteps. Abreu is a homer-hitting first baseman. He grew up in Cuba. Matt Davidson plays third base and is also a home run hitter. Shortstop Tim Anderson steals a lot of bases. The top pitchers are **starters** Lucas Giolito and Carlos Rodon.

◄ *Abreu has had three seasons with 30 or more homers. He moved from Cuba to play in Chicago.*

GEARING UP

Baseball players wear team uniforms. On defense, they wear leather gloves to catch the ball. As batters, they wear hard helmets. This protects them from pitches. Batters hit the ball with long wood bats. Each player chooses his own size of bat. Catchers have the toughest job. They wear a lot of protection.

THE BASEBALL

The outside of the Major League baseball is made from cow leather. Two leather pieces shaped like 8s are stitched together. There are 108 stitches of red thread. These stitches help players grip the ball. Inside, the ball has a small center of cork and rubber. Hundreds of feet of yarn are tightly wound around this center.

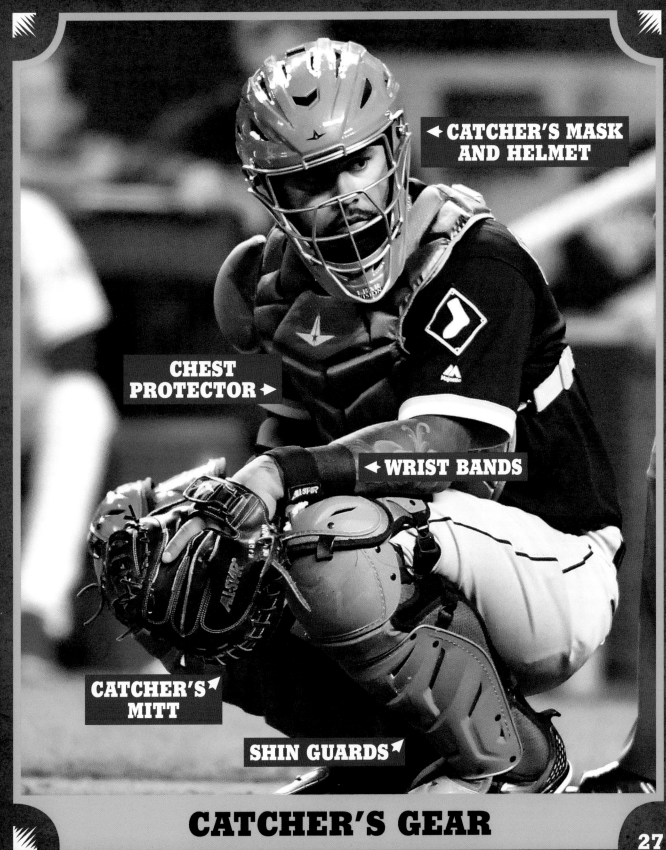

CATCHER'S MASK
AND HELMET

CHEST
PROTECTOR

WRIST BANDS

CATCHER'S
MITT

SHIN GUARDS

CATCHER'S GEAR

TEAM STATS

ere are some of the all-time career records for the Chicago White Sox. All these stats are through the 2018 regular season.

BATTING AVERAGE

Shoeless Joe Jackson	.340
Eddie Collins	.331

RBI

Frank Thomas	1,465
Paul Konerko	1,383

STOLEN BASES

Eddie Collins	368
Luis Aparicio	318

STRIKEOUTS

Billy Pierce	1,796
Ed Walsh	1,732

WINS

Ted Lyons	260
Red Faber	254

SAVES

Bobby Thigpen	201
Bobby Jenks	173

Paul Konerko was a hard-hitting first ➤
baseman for 16 White Sox seasons.

HOME RUNS

Frank Thomas	448
Paul Konerko	432

GLOSSARY

banned (BAND) prevented from ever taking part again

guaranteed (GARE-un-TEED) promised

Hall of Fame (HALL UV FAYM) a building in Cooperstown, New York, that honors baseball greats

mascot (MASS-kot) a costumed character that entertains sports fans

perfect game (PER-fekt GAYM) a game in which the starting pitcher wins and does not allow a single baserunner

rivals (RYE-vuhlz) two people or groups competing for the same thing

starters (STAR-terz) pitchers who regularly begin games

World Series (WURLD SEE-reez) the annual championship of Major League Baseball

FIND OUT MORE

IN THE LIBRARY

Connery-Boyd, Peg. *Chicago White Sox: Big Book of Activities*. Chicago, IL: Sourcebooks, Jabberwocky, 2016.

Gilbert, Sara. *World Series Champions: Chicago White Sox*. Mankato, MN: Creative Paperbacks, 2013.

Gutman, Dan. *Shoeless Joe & Me*. New York, NY: HarperCollins, 2009 (a novel).

ON THE WEB

Visit our website for links about the Chicago White Sox:
childsworld.com/links

Note to Parents, Teachers, and Librarians: We routinely verify our web links to make sure they are safe and active sites. So encourage your readers to check them out!

INDEX